A Banquet Seat
And
A Listening Ear

A Banquet Seat
And
A Listening Ear

stories from the kingdom frontiers

Dr. Bill Atwood

Ekklesia Society Publications
© 2019

A Banquet Seat and a Listening Ear
stories from the kingdom frontier

ISBN 978-0-9889552-9-5
© *2019 Dr. Bill Atwood*

Published by Ekklesia Publications
Printed in the United States of America
Edit and design by B. Lee Ligon-Borden

FOR INFORMATION
Dr. Bill Atwood
Ekklesia Publications
P. O. Box 5343
Frisco, Texas 75035
www.ekklesia.org
(800) 303-6267

Other Books by the Author

Here and Coming

The Spiritual Journey

Are we there yet?

Wild Vine: Fruitful Vine

Week after week, my whole family would dress up and head to church. We were an Army family, so we moved a lot, but somehow we always managed to find a chapel or a church. Eventually, I realized that all those years growing up, I had never missed Sunday school once. They used to give out perfect-attendance pins with little metal and enamel banners that would attach for each subsequent year. I used to joke that the medals would reach to my knees. My perfect attendance was for something like eighteen years! Sadly, in all those classes over all those years, I never knew that I could meet the Lord. It wasn't 'til later that I would come to actually meet Jesus. I can remember marveling that I had spent so much time in church, and so much time in Sunday school, yet never encountered Jesus personally.

I remember thinking, "Why didn't you tell me?!?" ...but the sad truth is, maybe they were just going through the motions, too, and couldn't share what they didn't have.

Now, years later, not only have I met the living Lord Jesus Christ, I have had countless experiences of encounters with Him. There have been more times than I can count when He has revealed himself, made the impossible possible, or led me through complex and even dangerous places with clarity—sometimes with such clarity it was almost as though He had spoken out loud.

This little book recounts some of those times. None of them happened because I'm special. They are all the result of Jesus being more special than can be described or imagined!

It is written with the hope that you, too,
will learn how to hear from Jesus Christ.

THE NATURAL WORLD

> ... *"What is your servant, that you should look upon such a dead dog as I?" (II Samuel 9:8)*

When we look at the world as it appears naturally, we are not actually seeing its natural state. The natural state of the world as it was created was perfect and resting in sweet intimacy with God the Father. What we see today, and assume is natural, is actually the fruit of rebellion – distortions resulting from sin that occurred in The Garden. We see the mess that sin has created and assume that what we see is not only the way things are, but also the way that they must be.

It's not surprising then, when people construct a worldview, it is flawed. After all, we are in a fallen place that is "wrong" and not true. A very common practice is to build a cosmology, or world view of how things work and how we should relate with God. A common world view is called the "orthodox wisdom position." What that means is that when we are good, we feel that we have earned God's love and he will bless us. When we sin or fail, we earn pain and punishment from Him. That sounds reasonable, but it's not right.

God's love for us is not dependent on us and what we do. It is based on Him and the way He relates with us. Perhaps the best Biblical story about this relationship is the story of Mephibosheth, the son of Jonathan, who was the son of King Saul, about 1,000 BC.

To understand the power of the story of Mephibosheth, one needs to know about covenants. The way King David treated Mephibosheth was not based on David's relationship with Mephibosheth; rather, it was based on David's relationship with *Jonathan*. How is that possible? It is because of something called a Blood Covenant that David and Jonathan shared.

A Blood Covenant is an agreement, but it is not like a contract. In a contract, two parties both enter into a formal arrangement that has three components: Performance, Compensation, and Agreement. If, for example, I am selling you a car, my Performance is delivering the car to you. My Compensation is the money I get. The type of car and the amount of money are specified in the Agreement. In that case, your Performance is giving me money. Your Compensation is the car, and the type of car and amount of money are based on what we have both agreed.

A Covenant is different. It is still an agreement, but in a Covenant, each party simply says, "I will do *this*." The *this* that I promise to do is unrelated to the performance of the other person. The "I will do *this*" that you promise, is unrelated to *my* performance on *my* promise. A Covenant is an oath before God. It is extremely serious. It is a vow that *must* be kept.

The added dimension of a Blood Covenant is that the two parties not only speak aloud their promises, but they do it in the presence of blood from an animal that has been sacrificed. This very graphically demonstrates that this Covenant is a really, really, serious occasion.

Again, although both parties declare their promises, each person's oath and promise is unrelated to the performance of the other. In other words, if we are in covenant together and you violate your promise to me, it does not release me from the Covenant I have made.

In this case, David and Jonathan killed an animal, then David and Jonathan joined hands and recited their Covenant Promises. We can read of the Blood Covenant that the two of them had:

Then Jonathan said to David, "Go in peace, since both of us have sworn in the name of the LORD, saying, 'The LORD shall be between me and you, and between my descendants and your descendants, forever.'" (I Samuel 20:42)

Here, it is important to note that the Covenant was "forever." That meant that even after Jonathan was killed in battle, David had the responsibility to care for Jonathan's descendants.

David asked, "Is there still anyone left of the house of Saul to whom I may show kindness for Jonathan's sake?" (II Samuel 9:1)

David called one of the servants who had served Saul, continuing his questioning:

Then the king said, "Is there not still someone of the house of Saul, to whom I may show the kindness of God?" (II Samuel 9:3)

The servant, Ziba, replied: "There is still a son of Jonathan who is lame in his feet." (II Samuel 9:3b)
David inquired where he was to be found:

And Ziba said to the king, "Indeed he is in the house of Machir the son of Ammiel, in Lo Debar."

Then King David sent and brought him out of the house of Machir the son of Ammiel, from Lo Debar. Now when Mephibosheth the son of Jonathan, the son of Saul, had come to David, he fell on his face and prostrated himself. Then David said, "Mephibosheth?"

And he answered, "Here is your servant!"

So David said to him, "Do not fear, for I will surely show you kindness for Jonathan your father's sake, and will restore to you all the land of Saul your grandfather; and you shall eat bread at my table continually." (II Samuel 9:4-7)

It's important to mention the context. Though we know more now about the character of God, at that time, the Jews thought that someone who was physically disfigured was in that condition because either they or their parents had sinned. As a result, Mephibosheth was not allowed to enter the synagogue. He was considered a sinner and an outcast. He was relegated to living on charity in a far corner, away from everyone familiar. I imagine him living in the storeroom of his uncle's store in Lo-debar. Lo-debar in Hebrew means "no pasture," or "no word, or no communication."

The meaning is clear. Mephibosheth was an outcast, living on the charity of someone called Machir, the son of Ammiel, in a remote location we might refer to as "the boondocks." He was so used to being an outcast that he couldn't believe it when he heard the proclamation of King David that the King would "restore to you all the land of Saul your grandfather, and...eat bread at my table continually."

He was in disbelief, and his self-image was broken.

Then he bowed himself, and said, "What is your servant, that you should look upon such a dead dog as I?" (II Samuel 9:8)

What he didn't realize was that his status was not determined by his life, character, performance, or circumstances; rather, it was determined by the Blood Covenant that the king had made with his friend Jonathan!

"As for Mephibosheth," said the king, "he shall eat at my table like one of the king's sons." Mephibosheth had a young son whose name was Micha. And all who dwelt in the house of Ziba were servants of Mephibosheth. So Mephibosheth dwelt in Jerusalem, for he ate continually at the king's table. (II Samuel 9: 11-13)

In great Hebrew fashion, the story ends with an exclamation (best read with a heavy Yiddish accent):

> *And he was lame in both his feet!* ("!" added!)

The narrator is all but overwhelmed that an outcast cripple, who by all rights would normally have been killed by a new king in order to eliminate the previous king's bloodline, was given the great riches of his grandfather's holdings. It is absolutely unbelievable in human terms. Mephibosheth was accepted not because of who he was and what he had done, but because of the Blood Covenant David had with Jonathan, his father!

But here is the best news of all…

Imagine that a voice cries out in heaven as God the Father cries out, "Is there anyone else from the household of my Son Jesus to whom I might show kindness for the sake of the Blood Covenant I have with Jesus, my Son?"

Then imagine what the answer to that question is! Can you hear the voice of an angel saying,

"Yes, Father, there is! There is one meant to become a Spirit-born son, a Spirit-born daughter."

In response to the Father, the angel calls out *YOUR* name!

Of course, we may have the reaction that Mephibosheth had, "What is your servant, that you should look on a dead dog as I?" but that is not the way God sees us!

If we have been joined to Jesus Christ by faith, the Father does not see us as morally compromised sinners. He sees all those in Christ exactly the same way that He sees His Son, Jesus! This is amazing good news! No longer are we seen as separated from God by our sin. We are seen as joined with Christ and presented to the Father wrapped in the righteousness of Christ.

Not only that, but He also invites us to His Table, the Eucharistic Table (Communion) now, and "in the age to come," He has secured a place for us at His Great Banquet Table in heaven!

All we have to do to receive this promise, is *receive* it! We don't have to earn it, deserve it, clean up for it, or do anything for it except *receive* it! Like Mephibosheth, we, with our broken, lame, sinful lives, give ourselves to Him along with all our junk. What we get in return is not based on the quality of what we offer, it is based on the quality of the Blood Covenant that the Father has with His son, the Lord Jesus Christ.

You can actually receive this right now, simply by praying and receiving the new life He has for you. You can pray a prayer something like this:

> Lord Jesus, I need you! I repent [turn from] my sins. Thank you for loving me and forgiving me. Thank You for pouring out Your life into the death that I deserved, as You fulfill the Blood Covenant of forgiveness with the Father. I give You my life and receive Your forgiveness and the new life that you won for me through the Cross and Resurrection. Thank you for giving me a place at the Father's Table. I receive this new life and commit to live my life as an offering of thanksgiving, serving you in the fellowship of the Church. And I pray this in Your Name, Lord Jesus. Amen.

If you have prayed that simple prayer, you have received new life in Christ. You have become a joint heir with Christ and have secured a place at His Table as His son or daughter.

It is important to walk in obedience to Him as Savior and Lord, doing the things that He has taught in Scripture. That means being part of a local church body where we learn about becoming part of the Body of Christ. We live our lives not as a way to win His acceptance, but as a 'thank you' for what He has done for us! If you have not been baptized, you should seek understanding about that powerful act, which is both symbolic and supernaturally powerful, and seek to be baptized as soon as you can arrange it.

It is also important for you to have a relationship with other Christians in a local church where you can learn and grow. Jesus calls us into covenant community where we can become more like Him.

Welcome to the family of God!

THE SHEPHERD'S VOICE

"My sheep hear my voice." (John 10:27)

The New Testament of the Bible begins with the four Gospels. When they were written, they were a revolutionary new kind of literature. They presented the life and ministry of Jesus Christ in ways to both comfort and challenge us. The Gospels are filled with wonderful information about Jesus. There are riveting stories, and theological truths. All of it is rich and valuable, but perhaps the most encouraging truth of all of them is that Jesus promises to speak to us. He is neither absent nor silent!

In John, Chapter 10, we read what is called the Good Shepherd Narrative. It is where Jesus describes Himself as The Good Shepherd.

"Most assuredly, I say to you, he who does not enter the sheepfold by the door, but climbs up some other way, the same is a thief and a robber. But he who enters by the door is the shepherd of the sheep. To him the doorkeeper opens, and the sheep hear his voice; and he calls his own sheep by name and leads them out. And when he brings out his own sheep, he goes before them; and the sheep follow him, for they know his voice.

Yet they will by no means follow a stranger, but will flee from him, for they do not know the voice of strangers."

Then Jesus said to them again, "Most assuredly, I say to you, I am the door of the sheep. All who ever came before Me are thieves and robbers, but the sheep did not hear them. I am the door. If anyone enters by Me, he will be saved, and will go in and out and find pasture. The thief does not come except to steal, and to kill, and to destroy. I have come that they may have life, and that they may have it more abundantly. I am the good shepherd. The good shepherd gives His life for the sheep." (John 10: 1-11)

In this packed narrative, Jesus gives us a tremendous amount of information—revelation, really, about Himself and the Kingdom of God. Not only does He let us know that He is the Good Shepherd, He also tells us that He is *good*, and He has come to help us have abundant lives. He also promises that He will speak to us, and we can hear His voice.

"And when he brings out his own sheep, he goes before them; and the sheep follow him, for they know his voice." (John 10:1; emphasis added)

The voice of Jesus can be different from most voices we know. Most are from people who are around us that we hear, or voices we hear over phones or other devices. Jesus *can* speak just like that, but my experience is that He usually doesn't. That doesn't mean He is not speaking – it's just that He speaks in different ways.

What follows are some wonderful ways that the Lord has "spoken" to me. Often these incidents occur on what are called the "Frontiers" of ministry, places where the Gospel is unknown, or it is under assault. I've learned countless things about the Lord and His Kingdom in decades of travel over more than eleven million miles in the air.

SKULL AND CROSSBONES

Now the word of the LORD came to Jonah the son of Amittai, saying, "Arise, go to Nineveh, that great city, and cry out against it; for their wickedness has come up before Me." But Jonah arose to flee to Tarshish from the presence of the LORD. He went down to Joppa, and found a ship going to Tarshish; so he paid the fare, and went down into it, to go with them to Tarshish from the presence of the LORD. (Jonah 1:1-3)

The first way I'd like to address the Lord "speaking," is what is described as "the word of the LORD came to Jonah…"

My favorite flight mission while in the Air Force was Air-Evac flights. In these flights, we took planes to Frankfurt, Germany, got them re-configured for hospital patients, and then flew them back to the states to Andrews Air Force Base to go to Walter Reed Medical Center. The giant plane could be re-configured to carry eighty hospital litters! Usually, we had something like a dozen litter patients and thirty to fifty ambulatory patients who sat in regular airline seats.

On one of these occasions, we took off from Frankfurt with a bumper crop of litter patients – sixteen of them – and about fifty more ambulatory patients. The weather was bad in Frankfurt as usual; we hit the clouds at about 100 feet off the ground and stayed "in the soup" all through the climb. Right after we entered the clouds, I saw some blinking warning lights on the center console. They flashed on, and then went off before I could see what they were. That wasn't supposed to happen. There were often warning lights, but they were supposed to stay on when they were activated.

I asked the Flight Engineer if he had ever seen this happen before, where the warning lights flashed on and then went off again. He hadn't. No one on the crew had. I could feel a flutter in my stomach.

Facing a ten-hour flight across the Atlantic, I was very concerned. There were no places to stop along the way if we developed a problem. Every few minutes, there would be another flash of warning lights, but not the same ones. Different ones on the panel lit up, with a hundred systems being monitored. None of the lights stayed on.

I sat in my seat and thought about it, trying to think of some reason this could be happening. Eventually, I decided to pray. I closed my eyes and immediately "saw" in my mind's eye a pirate flag with a skull and crossbones. I could feel tightening in my chest.

When I opened my eyes and closed them again, I could not escape the powerful symbol that kept coming to mind. I knew it was "the word of the Lord" coming to me, even though I didn't know exactly what it meant! I was sure of one thing though: He was showing me that there were *bad* things coming. I knew the Lord was telling me not to cross the ocean.

With this "word" from the Lord, it became unthinkable to embark on an overwater flight that would go for hours with nowhere to land if a problem happened. In this case, I was all but certain that He was "telling" me that trouble was coming.

Shaken, I announced to the crew, "We are not crossing the pond with this undiagnosed problem. It is just not safe." As soon as I said that, I felt a flood of calm.

The co-pilot said, "Twenty-first Air Force and the Med-Evac Center at Scott AFB are going to be furious!"

"Don't care," I replied. "It may be a career killer, but I don't want to be a 'hospital patient killer.' Call them."

He got on the radio and delivered the news to the 21st Air Force Headquarters duty officer.

It had been morning in Frankfurt, but that meant it was still in the middle of the night in the United States. The duty officer was very agitated and said, "Tell the pilot that if he diverts, this is a "Close Watch" mission. That means, it's three o'clock in the morning and I will have to call and wake up a Three-Star General and give him the news that Captain Atwood is diverting an Air Evac mission. I wouldn't want to be in your shoes!"

"Go ahead," I replied. "You can fire me after we land, but this aircraft isn't crossing the ocean until we find out what is causing this problem." Again, peace returned.

Having no choice, they began to coordinate where we should divert that could handle all the patients on board. Before long, they radioed back that we needed to divert to Mildenhall RAF Base in the United Kingdom. There is a huge USAF hospital only about 15 minutes away from that base. We got a new clearance from air traffic control and headed for Mildenhall.

Just as we turned for our new destination, I looked down and the warning lights started coming on. This time, however, they stayed on, as several systems began to fail. More lights began flashing and more systems failed. We were extremely busy following checklist procedures to handle the loss of so many items.

Usually, when something fails on an aircraft, it is no big deal because there are so many redundant systems. This time, however, there were multiple failures that seemed unrelated. My chest constricted like a vise!

"Engineer, isolate the generators." My plan was to separate the four electrical generators, each of which was powered by jet engine. Normally, they all worked together, but I determined to separate them so they would not interact with compounding failures. It was a good plan—technically foolproof—but it didn't work. Even isolated, the four electrical systems kept having crossover failures that were technically supposed to be impossible.

"Co-pilot," I said, "Get on the horn and get a phone patch with engineering and see if they can figure out why these multiple failures are happening. This isn't supposed to be possible!"

Word came back shortly from the Lockheed engineer on call that from their standpoint what was happening was impossible. Only it wasn't impossible: it was happening. Every minute or so something else would fail. More warning alarms would go off as more and more systems failed.

Suddenly, the cockpit was plunged into darkness, as we were in heavy clouds. All the lights, intercom, radios, navigation computers, and radio aids were dead. Flying the aircraft was a very heavy task with no autopilot and no guidance equipment. In a few seconds, the emergency hydraulically powered standby generator kicked in, and we got a few emergency lights, one emergency radio, and the intercom between only the engineer and me.

You can imagine how my chest was tightening. I purposed to breath regularly. Other than shouting to the crew members who had lost even intercom connection, there was no way to communicate with anyone on the crew except the engineer whom I could reach on the emergency intercom. There was one emergency radio that worked only from my seat, so I was flying, communicating with the controllers over the radio, and diagnosing the situation with the Flight Engineer, desperately trying to figure out what was going on.

The navigator got up from his seat and came over to stick his head next to mine since his headset didn't work.

"Boss," he shouted, "Hate to add to the problems, but I looked at the radar just before it failed. We have solid weather all the way from where we are to Mildenhall. The ceiling is really low at the base…down to two hundred feet. With all our nav aids out, it is next to impossible to do an instrument approach."

"OK," I said over the intercom, but then realized that only the Flight Engineer could hear me. I slipped my headset back off my ear, flying with my other hand, and cried out to the crew at the top of my voice, trying to be heard over the aircraft noise. "I'm still planning on going to Mildenhall since that was our last clearance and course. Just pray that they are able to do a GCA approach!"

A GCA is a radar approach in which precision radar equipment determines the position of the aircraft and a controller on the ground gives instructions to the pilot over the radio. We were used to doing those approaches because we practiced them every month, but this one was different. Normally, the controller gives the pilot a compass heading, but this time all the compasses were out except for the emergency standby compass. It was usually called the "whiskey compass" because it was a magnetic compass that was floating in alcohol. The problem with the whiskey compass is that it is good only for general headings. It flops around too much to be used for a radar approach.

When instrument failure occurred, controllers came up with a "no-gyro" approach to guide the pilot from the ground when they couldn't tell their compass heading accurately. My flight instructor in advanced pilot training had insisted on my learning how to do a no-gyro approach, saying, "You never know when you might need to know that."

"Mildenhall approach, this is Air-Evac 8080. Be advised we are declaring an emergency. Total electrical systems failure. I'm down to interphone with the engineer and this radio to you. Co-pilot, Nav, and the rest of the crew are incommunicado. I've asked for a report from the Doc in back to see if there are any medical emergencies. We've got seventy-three souls on board. One hundred thirty thousand pounds of fuel on board."

I paused.

"Mildenhall approach…with total nav system failure, the only way I can get this plane through the weather is if you have an old-timer there who knows how to do a no-gyro GCA. Please advise."

A no-gyro GCA was a ground-controlled approach in which the controller steers the plane by telling the pilot to "Turn left. Stop Turn." Or "Turn right. Stop turn." By learning the pace at which the aircraft is turning, a good controller is theoretically able to guide the plane to the runway through terrible weather. The problem was that it was an outdated approach, replaced by other types of electronic guidance. It was a left-over from the Korean war, and only a seasoned veteran controller would even know what it was!

The tension in the cockpit was palpable. Although I was so busy flying and talking on the radio, fulfilling almost all the flight tasks myself, it did not distract me from the tightness in my chest. I could feel my heart pounding and even hear my pulse in my own ears.

A slow drawl came over the radio, "Air-Evac 8080, this is Chief Master Sergeant Walters. I'm the chief controller here at Mildenhall. I can do a no-gyro for ya. I'm gonna get you on the ground safe and snug. Copy?"

"Roger that, Chief. WONDERFUL to hear you! Thanks for the help. I'll also need no-gyro guidance to the airport to line up for the approach since all our nav aids are out. Can you do that?"

"Sure thing, Son. No worries. Let's learn to dance."

I knew what he meant. As the radar controller gave instructions to turn or stop turning, each pilot carried out that instruction at a slightly different rate. The controller needed to learn the rhythm of the pilot's turns responding to the instructions that were given. After three or four turns, the Chief Master Sergeant said, "Ok, Son. Let's get you on the ground."

This was very unusual. The no-gyro instructions, which usually were given only on the final approach to landing had to start at high altitude. The veteran controller had to extrapolate the information on his RADAR screen on a regular scope that was far less precise than the precision one designed to guide a pilot in the last part of landing.

Sounding as calm as if it were a Sunday picnic, the Master Sergeant gave me turning and descent instructions as we flew blind through the clouds. Tensions were palpable in the cockpit because I couldn't tell anyone but the Flight Engineer what was going on over the intercom, and I was too busy to shout out updates to the crew.

On the descent during a part that was not as busy, I called out to the other crew members in the cockpit to tell them what was happening and asked them to brief the flight surgeon and the lead Air-Evac nurse in the back of the plane. They were trained to give the necessary briefings to the patients and passengers, and to get everyone ready for the emergency landing. With total electrical failure, the "Scanner," (a second Flight Engineer) would have to lower the landing gear manually from the equipment bay under the cockpit and through windows in the side of the plane where the passengers and patients were. Without the PA system, they would have to get close to the people and make the announcements several times throughout the patient area.

Physically, flying the plane without the electronic equipment was very fatiguing. Adjustments to different speeds and flight descents gave a different feel to the aircraft each time a change was made. Normally, this change was easily adjusted with buttons on the control yoke. Now with no electrics, trim adjustments had to be made with a big lever that moved hydraulic controls. The complexity, unfamiliarity, and danger made for a tense environment. Having so many people close-by only added to the tensions. It was like a metal band around my chest, but years of excellent Air Force training had me pretty well convinced that this was possible.

Through turning and descending, "The Chief" on the other side of the radio kept us informed of our position relative to the airfield. For us, there was an unchanging view of grey fog out the windows.

"Air-Evac 8080, Mildenhall Approach. You are cleared for the no-Gyro RADAR approach, Runway 29. Maintain three thousand, heading 250, approaching extended centerline course. Altimeter 30.15 inches. Wind 270 at 5. Recommend you configure prior to the descent point in five miles."

"Roger, Mildenhall, understand, cleared approach. Maintaining three thousand, heading 250, altimeter 30.15."

Then I called the Engineer on the intercom. "Send the Scanner to lower the gear now. Let everyone know that we are on approach. Let them know I'm praying, and they are welcome to join in praying!"

The Chief Master Sergeant's instructions continued to come in calmly and smoothly as he guided us through the clouds toward the runway.

"Air-Evac 8080, on course, on glide path. One mile from touchdown. Lookin' good."

"Air-Evac 8080, tower advises you are cleared to land runway two niner. Ceiling 100 feet. Visibility Runway Visual Range one thousand two hundred feet at the surface. Wind 270 at 5. Altimeter 30.15...Good luck, Son."

"Roger, Mildenhall. Cleared to land two niner. Altimeter 30.15. Thanks for the great help. Hope to lay eyes on you once we're on the ground!"

"Roger, Air-Evac. See you shortly."

"Runway twelve o'clock, altitude three hundred feet. On course, on glide path. No need to acknowledge...cleared to land Runway two niner. Wind 250 at 5. Two hundred feet. Approaching decision height in one hundred feet. At Decision Height, declare runway in sight or execute GO AROUND. Advise"

"Runway in sight, 12 o'clock. Thanks, Chief!"

With the nearly calm winds, the giant aircraft smoothly rolled onto the runway. With no electrics, the only way to steer was with differential breaking, applying breaks to one of the wheels so the airplane would turn that direction. Surrounded by emergency vehicles with countless flashing lights, we were able to clear the runway.

"Mildenhall Ground, Air-Evac 8080 clear of the runway. With all the equipment failures we've had, I think I need to stop this thing on the taxi-way and start getting patients into the ambulance busses rather than taxiing to the ramp."

"8080 you are cleared to stop there and shut down. Equipment approaching. Welcome to RAF Mildenhall. Really well done, Sir."

'Thanks, Mildenhall. Shutting down. Be advised when the engines shut down, we will lose hydraulic power. That means I will lose this last radio. I'll wait till the fire crew is on board with a radio before I pull the plug."

As we sat on the taxiway, it was like everyone on the crew let out a big sigh of relief at the same time! I could feel the tension from adrenalin draining out of my body and being replaced with a flood of peace. Unfastening my seatbelt and shoulder harness, I turned around and saw everyone on the crew smiling broadly.

"Hey, Boss. Great job. THAT'S what we train for! Well done."

"Great job, everyone," I exclaimed. "Let's get these patients to Lakenheath and look at this sky-pig and try to figure out what happened!"

Before getting up from my seat, I stopped, bowed my head, and said aloud,

"Thank You, Lord, for Your word of guidance—for showing me that danger was coming and leading me to bring all these people to safety. Thank You for Your word and Your great love!" When I looked up, no one was phased by the prayer. They were all smiling and nodding in agreement.

Clamoring up the ladder into the cockpit was a big guy with *lots* of stripes on his sleeve. "Where's the AC?" (Aircraft Commander)

"That's me," I replied. "You Chief Walters?"

"Yes, indeed!" He exclaimed as he wrapped his arms around me in a bear hug. "Son, that was really well done. You did great.

"No disrespect meant by the hug, Sir."

"No problem, Chief. You certainly earned a hug and more! That was an amazing descent and approach. You're just a young buck, Sir. Where'd you learn No-Gyros? That's an old-timer's approach!"

"My flight instructor in T-38 fighters was an old fighter F-100 pilot. He insisted I learn them. Said I'd probably need to know how some day. Seems like he was right."

The Flight Engineer came back up into the cockpit, "You're not going to believe this!! You know, all four electrical systems are independent. When they're in isolated mode, there is no interconnection at all. What happened with all these failures should have been impossible. What no one thought of is there is a place where all four systems physically come together. Even though they are not connected, each one passes through a junction box. The four junction boxes are stacked one on top of the other.

"Unbelievably, we had a failure on system one. That led to an electrical fire that started melting metal. It got so hot that molten metal dripped from one system to the one below it, spreading the fire from one system to the other until it wrecked all four "independent" electrical systems!. Without fear of contradiction I can say that was a huge design mistake!! That's why we lost everything."

At this point, the Command Post Duty Officer climbed into the giant cockpit. "Good news for you, Captain. With all the equipment failures, 21st Air Force has decided you are not an irresponsible troublemaker, after all. They are pretty pleased that you got this thing on the ground with all these failures....Even with all the trouble with moving patients. Looks like you are going to skate from getting in trouble!"

Imagine what had happened. The "word of the Lord" had come to me from the picture of a pirate flag of a skull and crossbones had spoken to me clearly, and that guidance had saved all our lives.

As the great evangelical writer Francis Shaffer said, "He is there, and He is not silent!"

STILLING OF THE STORM

But the LORD sent out a great wind on the sea, and there was a mighty tempest on the sea, so that the ship was about to be broken up. (Jonah 1:4)

The temperature on the ramp was 132° F. I was in command of a mission from Saudi Arabia to Tehran, Iran. It was the time of the Shah of Iran before he was ousted by fundamentalist Islamic clerics. I often flew through the Middle East carrying mail and priority cargo for embassies and consulates. I always smiled because the standard "op order" directing our mission and movements always carried the instruction that we were to fly in civilian clothes rather than in uniform. I'm sure our civilian garb *completely fooled* everyone into thinking that the super clean-cut guys who climbed down the aircraft stairs of a 325,000-pound plane with a giant flag and letters on the side saying "US AIR FORCE" were just average civilian cargo pilots! In any case, it was probably less obvious that we were military when we went into the terminal or flight operations, although we spent a lot of time joking about hiding our plane with science fiction "cloaking" devices.

On this particular mission, we had been diverted into Dhahran, Saudi Arabia, to pick up extremely high priority cargo that, because of its content, was marked "PAX Pro." That means it was prohibited to carry passengers on a flight with that cargo. From there, we were to fly to Tehran, Iran, to deliver our high priority cargo. After our flight plan was filed and we went back to the plane to get it ready for take-off, a military ambulance raced across the tarmac and pulled up by our plane.

A doctor jumped from the ambulance and ran over to me. "You the AC? [Aircraft Commander] I have a patient here with a failing heart. We can't treat him here. If I can't get him to Tehran in the next ten to twelve hours, he will certainly die. Thank God you are here! I heard you are going to Tehran!"

At this point, the Duty Officer in charge of operations at Dhahran jumped in, "Sorry, Doc, we just put super-high priority cargo on board and it's PAX Pro. Your guy can't go."

Not surprisingly, this made the doctor really mad and he turned to me, "Surely you are not going to let this patient die because of paperwork!"

I said, "Let me get 21st Air Force on the horn and see if they'll give me a waiver. Let's try to get your guy to Tehran."

We raced back into the terminal to find out that the special secure phone line to the Headquarters in the United States was not working. At that point, we all jumped back in a van to go back to the plane.

"Let me try to get through to 21st Air Force Head-quarters on HF [the long-range, short-wave radio]," I said.   From the cockpit, we were unable to contact anyone. I could feel drops of sweat rolling down my back and felt the desert heat getting to me.

 The Duty Officer (the ground support staffer who worked there in Dhahran) said, "I'm sorry, Doc, but I just can't let a passenger on the plane without a waiver. My career would be down the drain. I just can't break the rules."

At this point, I withdrew into my own thoughts and began to pray. The Lord reminded me of my grandfather and the kind of counsel he often offered. I knew exactly what he would say. It was almost like Jesus and my grandfather were standing right there. There was a way my grandfather would crook his fingers in a gesture that signaled to me he was going to offer wisdom. Here in my head was his familiar voice saying, "Regulations are guides to the wise, and bondage to the fool." In my mind's eye I could see the Lord smiling behind him. The tension in my chest began to lessen.

The designation of cargo as "PAX prohibited" is designed to keep people safe. They did not want people on the plane to be injured by dangerous cargo. Here, the principle of that which was supposed to keep people safe was just about to kill someone! That was not the idea!!

I reached over to the Duty Officer's clip-board and slid it from his hand. On the manifest, I wrote: "Passenger waiver for PAX Pro cargo issued by Captain W. G. Atwood, III," signed and dated it.

"You can't do that!" said the duty officer, while the doctor smiled.

"I just did. Look," I told him, "Your concern is your career and the rules. I just signed the papers and took responsibility for the decision. If the commanders get angry, it won't be with you. You have a 'Get Out of Jail Free' card with my signature, so I'm taking responsibility. No matter what, you'll be OK. Now, load the patient."

We loaded the patient and tied down the dangerous cargo and prepared for the hour and a half flight to Tehran. Within minutes, we were airborne and turning north toward Tehran. Naturally, we had checked the weather before taking off. The weather had been within limits. During our short flight time toward Tehran, I had the co-pilot check weather again. This time, the news was not good.

"Boss," the co-pilot offered, "weather at Tehran is deteriorating. There is a windstorm kicking up. In the last fifteen minutes a huge crosswind has kicked up from nowhere. Right now, it's coming off the mountains to the north at fifty knots. It's a direct cross to runway 27. Our limit is twenty-five knots. What do you want to do?"

"We still need to go there and try an approach. We need to get this guy on the ground or he's not going to make it. Let's set up for the approach and monitor things to see if we can get on the ground."

Something was stirring in my spirit. I could feel something rising, like the Lord was about to do something dramatic. I weighed whether or not to say something and decided that the Lord was prodding me to pray. I went back and forth with myself for a bit, but then decided to encourage the guys.

I keyed the intercom and said, "Ok...We really need to get this thing on the ground, and we really need to get this guy to the hospital. I'm going to pray for the wind to die down. Call Tehran approach and tell them that we'd like to shoot the approach and see if the wind is in limits when we get to the DH [Decision Height]."

The co-pilot called the approach controller and gave them the word on what we wanted to do. Coming back over the radio we heard, "Mac 70023, you are cleared approach." ("Mac" was our call sign for Military Airlift Command.) "Be advised that no aircraft have been able to land since this wind picked up. We don't know if we will be able to clear you to land with winds this high. Please acknowledge, you are cleared low approach only. Field is presently closed, with winds out of limits"

"Roger Tehran Approach. We'll give it a look and see. We confirm, low approach only unless further advised. Please keep calling out the winds for us during the approach." Then over the intercom, I said, "Landing gear down. Before Landing Checklist," and the co-pilot moved the lever to lower the landing gear.

Immediately, we felt a huge shudder and heard a tremendous bang. The hydraulic pressure went to zero on the number two system that operated the landing gear, and all kinds of warning lights and alarms started blinking. Again, I could feel tightness grip me.

"Scanner, Pilot," (the Scanner is a second flight engineer who is not in the Engineer's seat for that flight but handles things outside before take-off and things inside onboard when there are problems. The communications protocol was to say the position of the person you wanted to reach and follow it with your own position on the crew), "Please check it out, but it is pretty obvious we have lost Hydraulic System number two. See if the gear came down."

"Pilot, Scanner. Nose gear and left main gear are down. Right main is hung midway."

This was the most critical situation for landing imaginable. With one main landing gear down and the other not deployed, on landing the plane would tend to drag the side without a wheel and begin to pivot in that direction. Such a situation usually resulted in the plane not only spinning, but tumbling end over end. It really needed to be addressed, and quickly!

"Initiate manual gear extension checklist and try to get all the gear pinned as quickly as possible," I instructed. "I'll continue the approach. Co-pilot, call it in and declare an emergency. Check the wind again."

We were flying in a long box pattern that would parallel the runway, turning from one radio aid to another. The approach would take us past the end of the runway, extending east of the field. That gave plenty of time for the Scanner to pull the levers that caused the landing gear to drop into place, even when there was no hydraulic pressure moving them. Eventually, the approach would turn us north toward the extended centerline of the runway and then turn us left onto final approach back to the west, hopefully for landing on the West 27 runway.

As we flew along, the tower acknowledged our emergency. The flight engineer came back on the intercom after a few minutes, and said, "Confirming manual gear extension checklist complete. All three gears down and pinned in place."

Extending extra far to the east to give us more time to be stabilized, we eventually turned north and flew for a while until we were intercepting the final approach course. Tehran Approach kept calling out the wind.

"Mac 023, Merhibad Tower, wind 350 at 45." That meant that the wind had turned a few degrees and dropped by 5 knots, but still 20 knots outside our landing limits.

As we turned onto the base leg, 90° from the final course, tower called again, "Mac 023, Tower. Wind 350 at 40."

The loadmaster in the back of the plane couldn't hear the radios. He clicked on and said, "How's the wind?"

The co-pilot answered, "It's moving some and dropping. 350 at 40. Still too high."

"Pilot, Loadmaster."

"Go ahead, Load."

"Keep praying Boss. I've never lost a passenger. Don't want to start. Get this thing on the ground!"

"I am. Let's see what happens."

I was praying silently, but fervently, "Lord, save his life. Drop the wind. Help us get him to the doctors on the ground."

"Tehran Tower, Mac 70023 base, turning final."

"Roger Mac. Wind 340 at 40 knots. Field is still closed, but the wind is improving."

"Wind 330 at 35. Wind almost in limits. Will advise if we can clear you to land."

"Roger, Tower, copy. We'll continue the approach."

"Tehran Tower, Mac 70023. Manual gear extension complete. Confirming gear down and locked. Field in sight. Say wind."

"Wind, 300 at 35. Crosswind component within limits, field is now open. Continue approach. Will advise."

"Roger, Tehran. Be advised we have critical medical patient on board. Please dispatch rescue to pick him up as soon as we get on the ground. Have to get him to the hospital."

"Roger Mac. Equipment rolling. They'll be at the end of the runway on rollout. You are three miles final. Wind 270 at 30. No crosswind. You are cleared to land. Good luck."

"Roger, Tehran. Mac 023 cleared to land. Field in sight. Thanks!"

We touched down and rolled straight down the runway. Without brakes, I used the reverse thrust to slow the plane, pulling the levers to open big clam shells on the engines to make the thrust stop us. Now the wind that had been our worst enemy had turned. As it blew against the nose of the plane, it was helping to slow us down. As I pulled back the power on the reverse thrust, I could feel the power of the anxiety lessening as well. We came to a stop after a long roll out, stopping with only a few hundred feet of runway remaining.

"Mac 023. You are cleared to stay on the runway until we organize a tow. Be advised that the wind has shifted again. Wind currently 360 at 50. You had amazing timing. The field is now closed again."

The co-pilot exclaimed over the intercom, "Boss, did you hear that!?! The wind just dropped for us to land. Now it's back up to 50 knots and the field is closed again. That's amazing! Not only that, without brakes, having the wind on the nose of the plane when we landed was even better than having them calm. This is amazing!"

It was just sinking in how profoundly the Lord had blessed us. I sat shaking my head and thinking about what He had done. From a crosswind out of limits, and a closed field, to a best case, right down the runway to help us land and then slow down, He had provided what we needed. More importantly, He provided what our ailing passenger needed to save his life. My spirit was exhulting!

I heard a click on the intercom but no voice. Someone had keyed their intercom mike, but had not spoken yet... Eventually I heard, "Hey Boss. Pretty impressive."

Pretty impressive indeed, but I was not the impressive one, it was the King of Kings and Lord of Lords, the Master of the wind and waves. He had shown Himself to be the impressive one. Even the wind and the sea listen to him!

> *So they picked up Jonah and threw him into the sea, and the sea ceased from its raging. (Jonah 1:15)*

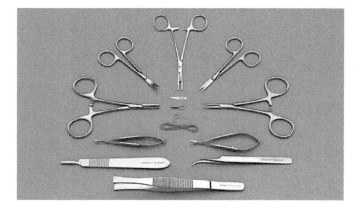

OPHTHALMOLOGICAL "MISTAKE"

But with the voice of thanksgiving I will
sacrifice to you; what I have vowed I will pay.
Deliverance belongs to the LORD!" (Jonah 2:9)

Years ago, when I first started traveling extensively in Africa, many things were not as they are today. For instance, these days, there is cell phone coverage almost everywhere. Back then, however, the only ways to communicate were by the undersea telephone cable from the capitals of some African nations, through Paris, then to an operator in New York. Once connected (and there was usually a five- or six-hour wait to get through to New York!), they would dial through to your number.

Medical care was challenging, as well. Many doctors were actually well trained, but there was a paucity of supplies. If someone needed surgery, the hospital would give that person a list of items to gather. Once the necessary supplies – from IV fluid and prescriptions to suture kits – were assembled, the patient could return to the hospital for the surgery!

I had a team of supportive physicians who got together to figure out, from the places I was traveling (like rural Nigeria!), what were the most likely problems to occur that were potentially lethal. They then compiled the necessary medications and supplies. Each time I went to one of those places, I would take a medical kit with drugs, supplies, suture kits, and even IV needles and tubes.

On one occasion, when I stopped by the clinic near my home to pick up my kit, the doctor had a big brown bag of supplies.

"One thing," he said. "When I was looking at the things I pulled for your kit, I realized that something had been misfiled. Instead of regular suture kits, one of them is an ophthalmological suture kit – for eyes. It's more trouble than it's worth to figure out how to re-stock it, so I just threw it in the bag with the other stuff."

I didn't think anything about it again and set off for Nigeria.

On this trip, I was in a rural area. I'd been doing Biblical teaching with clergy and had just preached at several very long and very lively church services. Pretty well exhausted, I was relaxing at the home of Dr. Nwabueze Magulike. Nwabueze means "Before the King." In other words, he was given a name calling him to live his whole life "Before the King," serving Jesus. His Igbo tribe delights in giving names that shape people's lives and seek to honor God. "Nwabu" is a delightful and dedicated eye surgeon, and a deeply committed Christian. As we sat on giant sofas with our feet propped up, our reverie was interrupted by the phone ringing.

My host (and friend) answered the phone, and I could hear him saying, "Oh, too bad. I guess I'll have to take it out."

"Nwabu, what's the problem," I asked.

"A young man has punctured his eye. Doesn't sound too bad, but since I don't have an ophthalmological suture kit, I'll have to take his eye out."

At first I felt a shudder of revulsion thinking about the eye being damaged, but then remembered what I had!

"Not to worry, Nwabu. I have one in my bag."

"No, friend, this is not a regular suture kit. It is a special one for operating on eyes. The regular one won't do."

"Just a minute," I said. "I'll show you. What I have *is* an ophthalmological suture kit! You are welcome to it."

I ran to my bag and rifled through it until I found what I needed.

"Here you go. I thought it was added into my kit by mistake, but it seems that the Lord knew the need, and it wasn't a mistake after all!:

"Praise God!" cried the devout ophthalmologist.

"I'll hurry to the hospital and see if I can save the eye!!"

And he raced out the door with suture kit in hand. About four hours later, he returned, beaming with a giant smile.

"It was perfect.," He reported. "The patient had been working and lost his grip on a sharp tool and pierced his eye. Without your suture kit, I would surely have had to remove the whole eye. He would have lost it forever. With this kit, I was able to stitch the eye and save it. He will completely recover. His normal vision will be restored. It is amazing that the Lord knew what we would need before we did! It looked like a mistake, but my God never makes mistakes!"

In Igbo tribal homes, many finish the day with family devotions. Dr. Magulike led the choruses of praise before we went to bed.

It was a fine day when the Lord showed Himself strong, working even when we didn't know He was at work.

What a wonderful God!

BRIBES, CHALLENGES, AND A FLIP-PHONE

As my life was ebbing away, I remembered the LORD;
and my prayer came to you, into your holy temple.
(Jonah 2:7)

I was on a Swiss Air flight from Zurich to Lagos, Nigeria. Lagos is one of my least favorite places in the world. It is so hard and rough. There are thieves and robbers. There are muggers who would just as soon kill you as not, who are in league with taxi drivers. If you catch a cab, you may never get to your destination. Many people have been driven to a remote area and killed just for the cash they had on hand.

On a previous trip to Lagos, I had been accosted by a ten-year-old boy with no hands. He said, "My father cut my hands off so I would be a better beggar." A shudder of revulsion ran through me. How disgusting!

The place was like the wild west, but with corrupt sheriffs. I always arranged for someone to meet me at the airport door, but it could still be a gauntlet getting through all the corrupt airport officials demanding bribes to let you pass. My Christian friends in Nigeria had pleaded with me not to pay bribes. They see bribes as a cancer. I was determinedthat I would not pay bribes, no matter what.

On numerous occasions, immigration and custom officials, one after another, were demanding, "Do you have Naira for me?" (Naira is the currency used in Nigeria.)

I would usually say, "I love this country. I can't pay you. It would rob the soul of this nation."

When I had done that in the past, they would seem shocked, but they would back off. I had been into the Lagos Murtala Muhammed International Airport many, many times. I was praying and thinking about those experiences as we began our descent to land.

Here is an account of one of the times I was entering Nigeria. I wrote about it in my book, *Here and Coming: As it is in Heaven.*

As the aircraft began to slow and configure for landing, I had the sense that the Lord was speaking. I looked out the window to the wing and "saw" in the Spirit an angel sitting on the wing with long hair flowing behind in the wind. There was an internal buzz of anticipation in my chest.

Not audibly, but very clearly, the Lord "said" to me, "Get out your flip-phone and program in the switchboard number of the United States Embassy in Lagos." It was so clear, I knew it was the Lord.

I complied. I found the number that I had written down and programmed it into the flip-phone.

This time, as I passed through all the airport customs and immigration checks, I thought I had arrived without incident. No one at immigration or customs gave me any problem, and no one demanded a bribe!

Without any problem, I walked out the door of the airport rejoicing. I thought "This time, I guess I made it through without an incident." I even saw the person who was meeting me off in the distance and began to relax.

My joy quickly faded as a military police officer and some security force men in civilian clothes took me by the arms and began to hustle me off into the darkness at the side of the building. I was praying in the Spirit and crying out to the Lord (albeit silently!). Anxiety rose.

I was certainly thankful for having the number of the United States Embassy available as I was being spirited away to who-knows-where. I began thanking the Lord for the provision of His word that something dangerous was coming and I needed to be prepared.

While we were still in the glow of the overhead lights, I reached into my pocket and flipped my phone open. Carefully feeling around for the memory button, I pressed "send." On the first ring, imagine my relief to hear, "U.S. Embassy, Lance Corporal 'something-something.' (I missed his name). How may I help you?"

I had seen the nametag of the leader of the group. In an instant, the Holy Spirit told me exactly what to say, "Hello, U.S. Embassy. I'm an American citizen calling. I just landed at the International airport. I'm calling to let you know of the wonderful service that this Nigerian police officer, Captain So-and-So has provided to ensure my safety. I would like you to make a note of his name so that he can be officially thanked for his good service."

Instantly understanding what was going on, the Marine at the embassy (the sharpest and the best Marines guard the embassies) said, "Sir, I can have a squad of U.S. Marines there at the airport in less than ten minutes. Do I need to send them?"

"That won't be necessary, Lance Corporal. I just wanted to let you know of the 'good' treatment I have received. Nigeria can be very dangerous. People disappear. I think it is enough just to let you know who it was who met me as I came out of the airport and 'how well' he has seen to my treatment. Here, I'm passing the phone to him. Why don't you thank him on behalf of the United States of America!"

I handed the phone to the Nigerian Police Captain. He put it to his ear. I could hear talking on the other end but couldn't quite hear what the Corporal was saying. I'm pretty sure that it was something like, "Captain. We are so glad to have your name and that you are helping our citizen." He made it clear that they would not get away with maltreatment toward me in any way.

When the Captain gave the phone back, I went back on the call with the Lance Corporal. "Thanks, Corporal. Great job today! Bravo Zulu." (Bravo Zulu is a Navy expression meaning "Well done!" at the close of a mission.)

"Aye, aye, sir," replied the Marine. "Call us back if you need us." My internal anxiety changed to victorious peace!

Confounded by the knowledge that their leader's name had been given to the U.S. Embassy, the police officers had little choice but to thank me for being so gracious to them and let me go.

On each of the occasions I've experienced when there was significant danger, it was not the danger that made up my most poignant memories. It was the sweet, almost tangible, presence of the Lord right in the middle of deep spiritual conflict.

I have reflected on that experience (and many others) a thousand times. At the worst of these circumstances, He was not absent but profoundly present. He was there in such a way that once having experienced His presence, I hungered for more. It is like worship but more substantial – not just inspirational, but robust.

Experiencing God's presence in that way was seared into my heart and memory. Now, I long for it and look back upon it. It's like being homesick, even though it was only a moment in time.

More than memorable, the experience of the Kingdom far overshadows the memory of any dangers. It has captivated my heart and I miss it when it is absent.

Missionaries sometimes speak of something similar. Despite the dangers and the hardships of the front lines of mission work, it is a compelling place to be. It is as though the Kingdom of God bows down low from heaven and comes especially near the earth.

> *It seems that if you stand on tiptoe,*
> *your head will poke through so you can get*
> *a clearer view of what Kingdom life is like.*

SATELLITE PHONE AND PEANUTS

And the LORD God prepared a plant and made it come up over Jonah, that it might be shade for his head to deliver him from his misery. So Jonah was very grateful for the plant. But as morning dawned the next day God prepared a worm, and it so damaged the plant that it withered.
(Jonah 4:6-7)

I was sitting with a gentle-spirited Archbishop. We were drinking tea. Sitting quietly, we looked out the large windows onto the lush green of the compound around his office.

"I'm so glad you've come. I've been thinking a lot. You know, I'm Archbishop over several countries. Most of them are Muslim majority, but one has recently ramped up Sharia Law. Now, I can get a visa to visit the country, but I'm not allowed to speak or hold services. I was thinking... you have an American passport. Could you go for me and minister to the people? They are allowed to meet – at least for now – but we have to be very careful. I think it would be a great encouragement for them if you could go. You can meet with them and preach and teach. I don't think the government will even notice."

Silently, I thought, "Sharia Law! Oh, no!" as my chest tightened.

"Of course," I replied. "I'm glad to go for you."

"You will have to sanitize everything. No clergy collar, no vestments (church robes). Nothing Christian. You'll have to leave all those things behind, or you will be denied entry."

A couple weeks later, I was in a third country, where I had arranged to leave my "Christian things" at the hotel where I had been staying and headed to the airport. All was normal checking in and flying. As we were getting ready to descend, the flight attendant came around with a customs form and a landing card to fill out. My eye fell on the first question on the customs form:

"Do you have any electronics, cell phone, radio transmitting equipment, or a satellite phone?"

My heart fell. Because of years of travel to remote areas, I have carried a satellite phone as well as a couple of cell phones for Kenya and the USA. As I sat pondering what to do, I could "hear" the Lord's voice in my head, "It is better to declare what you are not supposed to have than to be found concealing it! But don't worry, I will tell you exactly what to do."

Then a scene unfolded in my mind. It was much like remembering a scene from a movie. Then the Lord spoke, albeit in silence, in my head. Quietly, but very clearly, "When you go into the arrivals hall, walk up to the inspector and take the hearing-aid out of your ear and hold it up. Say, 'Your form asked about electronics. I have these."

They will say, "No problem."

Then say, "I also have two cell phones. One for the USA and one for Kenya." There will be no response. But when you say, "I also have a satellite phone." All kinds of excitement will break out and you will be surrounded with people with guns. Don't worry. Just do as I tell you."

So, I did. "I also have a satellite phone."

It was as if a silent alarm had sounded. In seconds a circle of police with sub-machine guns all pointed at me, surrounded me. It took my breath away.

The Lord said, "They will ask, 'WHY do you have a satellite phone?' Here is what you say, 'I do development work in remote areas, often outside the cell system network. On my wedding anniversary, I was off network and I decided never to be unable to call again.'"

That's exactly what I said.

Beaming with a huge smile, the inspector got up and walked around the counter and slapped me on the arm, "Brother! You got to call the wife on your anniversary!! Welcome to our country!" With a big welcoming sweep of his arm, he motioned me through the inspection station out to meet my friends.

Exultation rose inside me as I went on to the hotel and met up with Christians there. We had a warm visit. When we gathered at the church building for me to speak, we had a lovely dinner of local cuisine and then people settled in for some Bible teaching.

I said, "I suppose you have trouble getting Bibles."

"No!" They replied and all held up their smart phones. "What version do you like to use? One of the advantages of the digital age is that they can't stop us downloading Bible apps!"

At the close of the meeting, I asked, "If you can get Bibles, what do you need?"

"Discipleship materials," several leaders replied with one voice. "We can get the Bibles, but it is hard to get discipleship materials. The next time you come, could you bring some?"

"Of course," I replied, but nervously wondered how I could. Importing Christian material was illegal.

As things worked out, I was going to be in the area the very next month, so I gathered a suitcase full of discipleship materials, and planned on taking them into the country for the Christians there.

I knew what to do about getting a satellite phone into the country, but this was a more challenging trip. This time, I had an entire suitcase full of banned Christian discipleship materials! Although I was confident that the Lord could navigate me through the gauntlet of entering the country, there was more than an undercurrent of fearful awareness of what could happen. For me, that often manifests as a tight feeling in my chest. I become more aware of my breathing, and when it is at its worst, I can feel my pulse pounding in my ears.

I was about to head to the airport from another country. I was standing in a convenience shop when the Lord "spoke" very clearly. It was not audible, but it was just that clear. I love the clarity with which the Lord speaks on these mission frontiers!

"Open your eyes!" the voice "said." It was like it was speaking without speaking.

"Lord, my eyes are open," I replied, quite confused.

"What do you see?"

Still puzzled at what was going on I replied, "I see peanuts…?" wondering if that is what He meant.

"Buy them." That was definitive!

I thought, "I'm getting in late. Maybe the hotel restaurant will be closed. Maybe I'll need a snack. Who knows!?!" I just knew I needed to buy the peanuts.

Onboard the plane, the flight attendant began passing out the arrival forms. "I know what to do with this," I thought. When I looked at the form, it was different from the one I had received just a month before. This time, the first question was:

"Do you have any plants, plant material, or anything that came from a plant? __Yes __No"

"Oh, my goodness," I thought. "Why yes I do! I have peanuts!" I didn't know why that was important, but I knew it was going to be. Anticipation was bubbling up.

When I entered the arrival hall, I had my regular suitcase, plus the bag filled with "illegal" Christian discipleship materials. I could almost smell the adrenalin. I was a bit nervous, but I was also excited to see what the Lord was going to do with His peanuts.

I walked up to the inspector, this time a woman in hijab. I held up the customs form and the bag of peanuts and said to the inspector, "Your form asks if I have anything that came from a plant. I have these peanuts."

Immediately, she swung her arm over the desk and grabbed the package of peanuts out of my hand. Then she stood up and with a very loud voice, cried out, "Attention in the arrival hall! Attention in the arrival hall!" Then holding the package of peanuts up she said, "This visitor has such respect for our laws, when we asked about plant materials, he even declared that he had these ground nuts!" (That's what they call peanuts there.)

She went on, "Everyone should learn from him! You should all have the respect for our laws that this man has!"

Then, she turned to me, handed the package of peanuts back to me and said, "Welcome to our country. No inspection." What an amazing response. It made my heart sing!

Obviously, the Lord knew I had all the discipleship materials that this nation had outlawed. He knew that if they inspected my bags, they would find them. At the very least, they would seize the materials and destroy them. At worst, I could be arrested. The penalties for such blasphemy could be very severe. With this word from the Lord, He had used a plant to do his bidding, just like what had happened with Jonah!

And the LORD God prepared a plant and made it come up over Jonah, that it might be shade for his head to deliver him from his misery. So Jonah was very grateful for the plant. (Jonah 4:6)

When I met with the Christians and told them the story, I held up the bag of peanuts ("ground nuts" to them). As I spoke, they got more and more excited. By the time I finished, they were standing on their feet, clapping and shouting, "Hallelujah!"

What a wonderful day!

HOT BUTTERED NAAN

I went down to the moorings of the mountains;
The earth with its bars closed behind me forever;
Yet You have brought up my life from the pit,
O LORD, my God.
"When my soul fainted within me,
I remembered the LORD;
And my prayer went up to You,
Into Your holy temple.
"Those who regard worthless idols
Forsake their own Mercy.
But I will sacrifice to You
With the voice of thanksgiving;
I will pay what I have vowed.
Salvation is of the LORD."
(Jonah 2:6-9)

Entering nations with draconian Sharia law taught me a lot about navigating across borders. Now, I've learned to always ask the Lord to show me exactly how He wants me to approach entering a nation. Rather than thinking that everything will be fine and expecting no problems, I have learned that in some dark lands, people whose lives are infected with evil demonic presences will sometimes respond with hostility to Christians, not because they are choosing to do so intellectually, but because the demonic presence is reacting to the presence of the Holy Spirit in the believer.

Having learned to be ready for that reaction, as well as many other potential problems (!), now I pray each time before entering any country and ask the Lord how I should approach the entry and also exactly what I should say.

As I was traveling to a country that has been getting increasingly hostile to Christians, I had prayed about entry as usual. This time, it was very clear what to say. I had that in the back of my mind as I approached the immigration desk. I had been to that very desk many times, and I had always been greeted in a very friendly manner. This time, however, I could tell there was a different atmosphere. There was something in the air that was severe.

We were arriving at 2:00 am, so it was not surprising that the immigration inspector was grumpy for having to be at work so late. As I walked up to the desk, the atmosphere seemed to get darker and darker. The inspector glared at me and said very sharply, "Why have you come to our country?!?"

I immediately tightened up. Sometimes in situations like this, I feel a tension gripping my gut—its almost like a vibration – nervous tension. The official was majorly exercised and sounded very harsh. As a result, I thought back to what the Lord had been showing me on the way there. And realized I had exactly what to say.

"Remember when you were little? When you came home from school and walked inside. As you closed the door, you could smell it. Coming from the kitchen your mother was baking hot, buttered Naan. Do you remember?"

The inspector, who moments before had been hostile, leaned back and closed his eyes, remembering the scene and the smell.

"Yes," he replied, "I remember," keeping his eyes closed. Never opening them, he inked the stamp on an inkpad and banged the stamp down on an empty page of my passport without even looking down.

Then, lost in reverie remembering the wonderful smell from his childhood, still without opening his eyes, he dreamily said, "Welcome to our country..." and motioned me in.

> *But I will sacrifice to You*
> *With the voice of thanksgiving;*
> *I will pay what I have vowed.*
> *Salvation is of the LORD." (Jonah 2:9)*

THE GOD OF THE SECOND CHANCE

The word of the LORD came to Jonah a second time,
saying, "Get up, go to Nineveh, that great city, and
proclaim to it the message that I tell you."
(Jonah 3:1-2)

Traveling through rural Kenya with my driver John, we were on a road that was somewhat elevated, with no "shoulders" on the side. Right at the edge of the tarmac (pavement), the ground just dropped away. The weather was hot, and the traffic was heavy.

As we drove along, I was thinking of what I would say in the teaching I was going to do in the remote diocese where we were headed. Looking up, across the road, I saw an old woman walking along, bent over with a huge load of sticks.

As we passed her, I remember thinking, "How exhausting!" The sticks were weighing her down, so she was bent over. She could not have made more than a few cents carrying them. I couldn't tell her age, but I knew she was not young. After gathering and cutting the sticks, she was carrying them to market to sell. It was a huge amount of work, more than I could imagine, especially for the miniscule return she would receive for doing it!

As we passed her, I felt the Lord's voice rising up from inside me. "Stop. Give her some money." It was not as strong as I was used to, so it took a while for me to realize that I thought the Lord was speaking to me.

Finally, when we had gone a bit farther, I said, "John, stop the car! I need to see that woman!"

John responded, "I cannot stop the car. The traffic is too heavy. There is nowhere to go. I will look for a place to turn around, but I can't stop here. The road is too narrow. and there are too many vehicles."

I agonized a bit as we drove on, thinking I had been slow to respond to the prompting of the Lord. As we drove, we got farther and farther away from the old woman and her great load of sticks. The tension in my chest was gripping, and my heart was racing.

"John, I said, "you have to find a way to turn around. I must see that woman."

But there was nowhere to turn. Many minutes passed before there was a small unpaved road intersecting the tarmac one on which we rode.

"Really, Bishop, do we need to go back?"

"Yes, John. Go back. The Lord is telling me to meet that woman."

As the cars and huge trucks whizzed by, it took even longer for us to find a break so we could pull back out onto the road to go back the way we came. Looking intently for the old woman, we saw nothing. We didn't see even a footpath where she might have exited the road, but she was nowhere to be seen. I felt the heavy weight of failure pulling my heart down. It weighed me down and was quite depressing. Looking and looking, eventually, we had to turn back on our original way without seeing her.

After I finished speaking, teaching, and ministering the next morning, we were headed back to Nairobi. As we drove along, I couldn't believe my eyes. Although we were miles away from where we had seen the old woman the day before, here she was again – at least it looked like her. Hunkered down and bent over, she was walking along carrying a big bundle of sticks.

I said, "John, look! God is giving us a second chance! Pull over! Stop the car!"

As I walked over toward her, she kept shuffling along, bent down. I couldn't imagine how heavy the load was that she carried. She didn't stop; she just kept moving along, more shuffling one foot in front of the other than actually walking.

I came up to her and spoke in Swahili. "Habari ya kazi?" That was a fitting Kenyan greeting for this situation. Literally it means, "How is your work?"

Kenyans will never tell you that life is hard or that their work is terrible. At worst, what they will say is "Hamsini, hamsini." Literally 50/50. What they mean is that some things are good, and some things are bad, but it is considered rude to tell someone else that you are struggling!

When she replied, "Hamsini, hamsini," I chuckled. Life was hard indeed for her not to say all was well, "Nzuri."

I reached into my pocket and pulled out a 1000 Kenya schilling note. It was worth about $10 U.S. We were in an area where a laborer would consider himself well paid to receive 100 KSh, or about a $1 U.S. a day. 1000 KSH was a very notable amount of money. It is likely that she had never held a note that large before as she took it in her hand. When she realized what it was, it was amazing. This old woman, who had been bowed over, stood up straight and began to dance. She moved her feet around like she didn't have any weight on her back and gave a great smile – showing that she was missing several prominent teeth – saying over and over, "Asante, askofu! Asante, askofu!" (Thank you, Bishop, thank you, Bishop!")

We were in an area where the local language was Kamba, which I don't know. John, being Kamba, was able to speak with her. She spoke with sparkling eyes, and spoke, and spoke. Eventually, she paused, and he was able to translate.

"Bishop," (actually he spoke with his accent and he always pronounced it as "Bee-shop"), "You have given her a great testimony! She said that her daughter needs medicine. She is carrying these sticks in order to get the money to pay for it. The cost is 1100 KSh. See…she is showing the 100 KSh she had. She cannot wait to get back into the village to show how God has provided. She was afraid that it was going to take many days to get the medicine. She only gets a few shillings for each load of sticks she carries. Now she says, 'Through Bishop, God has provided the money I cried out to Him to supply! God is great indeed!!'"

In an amazing gift from the Lord, I was given a great second chance to be found faithful. The first time, I was just a little too late in asking John to stop the car and we were not able to find her when we eventually turned back. This time, perhaps the same woman, perhaps another just like her – I couldn't really tell – appeared as a gift from the Lord. She was blessed. I was blessed. Even my driver John was blessed and misty eyed. God comes a second time and helps us to be found faithful even when we have stumbled the first time He called us!

The second time God spoke to Jonah, he heard and obeyed.

Thank God for second chances!

PASS

*So the LORD spoke to the fish,
and it vomited Jonah onto dry land.
(Jonah 2:10)*

Archbishop David Gitari, the retired Primate of the Anglican Church of Kenya (ACK), died Monday, September 30, 2013. He was 76.

Gitari was one of those larger-than-life figures. He was absolutely courageous, brilliant, and committed to the implications of the Gospel in everyday life. He was marked for death by government hit squads and three times had to escape in the middle of the night when they came to kill him. One of the times, he escaped through the roof of his house and slipped into the jungle.

When I first met David Gitari, I expected to meet a giant, and I was not disappointed. What I did not expect, however, was how hysterically funny he could be – and regularly was. He would smile with a broad grin and then succumb to the volcanic laughter that was rising inside and erupt with belly laughter.

95

One day, we were sitting in his office with our feet propped up. We were surrounded by great piles of papers arranged in some cryptic filing system known only to him, when he commented, "President Moi used to try to kill me. Now he prays for my health and safety because he knows if anything – even an accident – befalls me, he will be blamed!"

Gitari became a dear friend. When the Provincial Synod in Kenya was considering my consecration as a Bishop, there were many questions because of the complexities. In addition to my work in Kenya, I was being deployed to gather congregations in North America linked to Kenya. There was a great deal of discussion about the plan. Eventually, the retired Archbishop sauntered to the microphone and said, "It's time. It's for the Gospel." The measure passed unanimously.

Appreciating humor like fine wine, over the years he would often say to me, "Atwood! Tell the story! Tell the story again!" He did that in many countries and places when we were together, punctuating meetings and gatherings of all sorts. Again, and again, I would tell his favorite story and he would laugh as though he had never heard it before, convulsing with mirth that drew everyone else into raucous joy.

Here is the story of the Lord's deliverance that gave Archbishop Gitari such amusement:

I landed in Nairobi at Jomo Kenyatta Airport, cleared through immigration, and was passing through customs when I was stopped by an obviously very drunk inspector. With the exaggerated speech of the inebriated, he shook his finger at me and demanded, "Mzungu!" (using the Swahili word for white man), "What is in that bag? I have all the power! You have no power. I can put you in jail!"

The situation was bad. I looked around for some assistance, but it was late at night. and there were no other customs people in sight. Standing there I prayed silently, "Help, Lord! What do I say?" I could feel the tension of the moment gripping my body.

I remembered the Scripture,

But when they deliver you up, do not worry about how or what you should speak. For it will be given to you in that hour what you should speak; for it is not you who speak, but the Spirit of your Father who speaks in you. (Matthew 10:19-20)

I took a deep breath and replied, "My clothes and personal items. If you put me in jail, my friend will come and visit me," I replied.

"Mzungu!" he said again weaving back and forth as he stood wobbly, "I have all the power! You have no power. I can put you in jail. What is in that bag?" he cried, pointing to my briefcase.

"My papers and my laptop. If you put me in jail, my friend will come and visit me," I replied.

"Mzungu, I have all the power! You have no power. I can put you in jail!"

I responded, "If you put me in jail, my friend will come to visit me."

Pausing, the inspector looked quizzically at me and asked, "Who is your friend?"

"Archbishop David Gitari," I replied.

Turning away, he waved his hand and said, "Pass."

At that point, Gitari would collapse in gales of laughter, drawing everyone else within hearing into the same.

I don't know how many times over the years he cried out, "Atwood, tell the story!" but it was many. The next time I'm in Nairobi, I'll remember him again and I'll tell the story.

> Dear Archbishop David,
> As you approach the pearly gates clothed in the righteousness of Jesus Christ your Lord, I imagine that you will remember "the story" and laugh as St. Peter says, "Pass."

Certainly, this deliverance was not as dramatic as being spit out from a big fish, but it was a deliverance all the same.

It still makes me smile.

YOUR BANQUET SEAT &
YOUR LISTENING EAR

*For God so loved the world that He gave His
only begotten Son, that whoever believes in Him
should not perish but have everlasting life.
(John 3:16)*

I hope you have enjoyed this little book. The point is that you, too, can have a place at the Banquet Table of the Lord, and you, too, can hear His voice.

Go back to the chapter about Mephibosheth. Remember that your relationship with God is not based on what *you* do. It is based on the Covenant that God the Father has with God the Son, Jesus Christ. You can have a relationship with Him because *He* has already done what is necessary to make sure you can!

Once you are in a relationship with Him, Scripture promises that you can hear His voice! (John 10:27)

If hearing God's voice sounds too hard, you may be setting the bar too high or focusing on the wrong things. Here are some simple steps where you can begin the process of hearing His voice:

Step One. Take at least five minutes to tell the Lord things that you appreciate about Him and the world that He has created. You can tell Him that you appreciate tasty coffee, air conditioning, your spouse, or puffy clouds on a sunny day. There is something about expressing appreciation that unlocks the voice of the Lord.

Step Two. Make the decision to believe that God actually speaks. If you don't believe that He can speak, it is all but impossible that you will hear His voice! You can decide to believe what the Bible says, that "My sheep hear my voice."

Step Three. Make the decision that you will obey Him when you hear His voice. Instead of that, what we often do is essentially say, "Tell me, Lord, what you want me to do and I will decide if the plan is a good one and whether or not I will obey." Why would the Lord speak in that circumstance? If you commit in advance that you will obey, you are setting the stage for Him to speak.

Step Four. Ask Him to speak. When you ask Him to speak, it is important to listen. He may speak to you with:

- A Word
- A Picture
- A Scripture
- A Name
- An Action

Then, when He speaks, believe in Him, and commit to follow through. It always helps to regularly encounter Him by seeking to meet him in reading the *Bible.*

Christians do not live solitary lives, but we live out our lives in community with other believers. They can help you refine hearing His voice and help you learn how to apply the Scriptures to verify that what you think you are hearing is Biblically faithful. You can find an unlimited treasure of information about Jesus in the Bible. It is the most abundant and most authoritative source of information about Him. Hearing God's voice is a great adventure. You can get better and better at it. From what I've shared in this little book, you can see that it is even possible to hear very specifically.

When He speaks, adventure will surely follow!